I Love
Oceans

By Lisa Regan
Illustrated by Mike Saunders

Miles
Kelly

First published in 2008 by Miles Kelly Publishing Ltd
Harding's Barn, Bardfield End Green,
Thaxted, Essex, CM6 3PX, UK

Copyright © Miles Kelly Publishing Ltd 2008

This edition printed in 2011

2 4 6 8 10 9 7 5 3

Publishing Director Belinda Gallagher
Creative Director Jo Cowan
Editorial Assistant Toby Tippen
Designers Sally Lace, Carmen Johnson
Cover Artworker Carmen Johnson
Production Manager Elizabeth Collins
Reprographics Stephan Davis, Ian Paulyn
Assets Lorraine King

ISBN 978-1-84810-038-1

Printed in China

ACKNOWLEDGEMENTS
Page 16 Ash Toone/Fotolia.com
All other images from the Miles Kelly Archives

British Library Cataloguing-in-Publication Data
A catalogue record for this book is available
from the British Library

Made with paper from a sustainable forest

www.mileskelly.net   info@mileskelly.net

www.factsforprojects.com

Contents

Great white shark

The great white shark is a fierce hunter. It preys upon seals, sea lions and tuna fish. Great whites glide through the ocean, then speed up to catch their prey. Measuring up to 6 metres in length, the great white is the biggest hunting fish in the ocean.

Dark-coloured skin on the shark's back helps to camouflage it. This means that it is hidden in the deep ocean waters.

The fin on the shark's back is called the dorsal fin. It helps the shark to balance and steer.

Sharks have good eyesight, excellent hearing and a great sense of smell to help them find food.

The sharp, pointed teeth have jagged edges like a kitchen knife. If a tooth snaps, a new grows to replace it.

Hitchhiker

Remora fish often attach themselves to sharks for protection from predators.

Giant octopus

This huge octopus hides in caves at the bottom of the ocean. It has eight long arms called tentacles. If it is chased by a whale or a shark, the octopus squirts out black ink to hide itself, and swims quickly away. It can also change its skin colour.

Sea monster

Like an octopus, a giant squid has tentacles. These huge sea creatures can be as long as a swimming pool!

To help it cling onto rocks, the octopus's tentacles, are covered in suction pads.

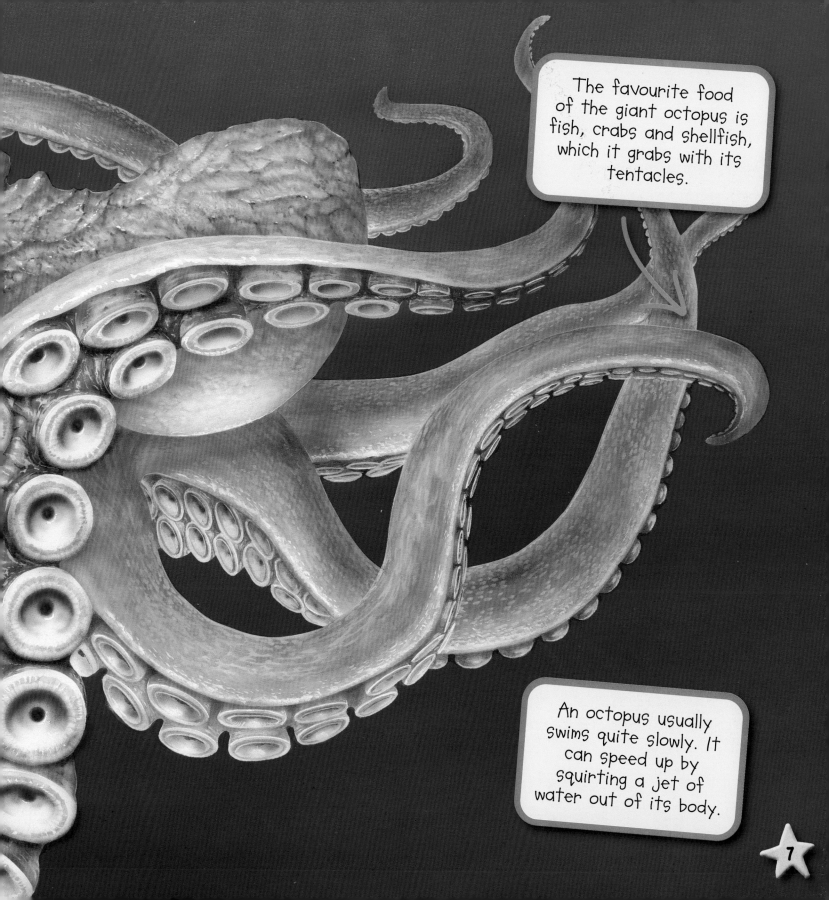

The favourite food of the giant octopus is fish, crabs and shellfish, which it grabs with its tentacles.

An octopus usually swims quite slowly. It can speed up by squirting a jet of water out of its body.

7

Thorny seahorse

Seahorses are actually fish, but they look very unusual. They have a horse-shaped head, a long body and a curly tail. Seahorses swim upright, bobbing through the water. To stay still, they wrap their tails around seaweed.

This fin helps the seahorse to swim. Other fish swim by using their tails.

Using their long snouts, seahorses suck up shrimps, small fish and other tiny creatures.

Baby seahorses hatch from eggs. The female puts the eggs in a pouch on the male's body. Four weeks later, the eggs hatch and tiny seahorses swim out.

Leaf disguise

The leafy sea dragon belongs to the same family as the seahorse. It is difficult to spot because it looks like a piece of seaweed.

The thorny seahorse gets its name from the sharp spines along its back.

Clownfish

Bright and colourful, clownfish live among coral reefs. They make their homes among the stinging tentacles of the sea anemone. Although it looks like a plant, the anemone is actually a meat-eating animal. It does not sting the clownfish, and in return the fish keep the anemone clean.

A slimy coating called mucus covers the body of a clownfish. The mucus protects the fish from the anemone's stings.

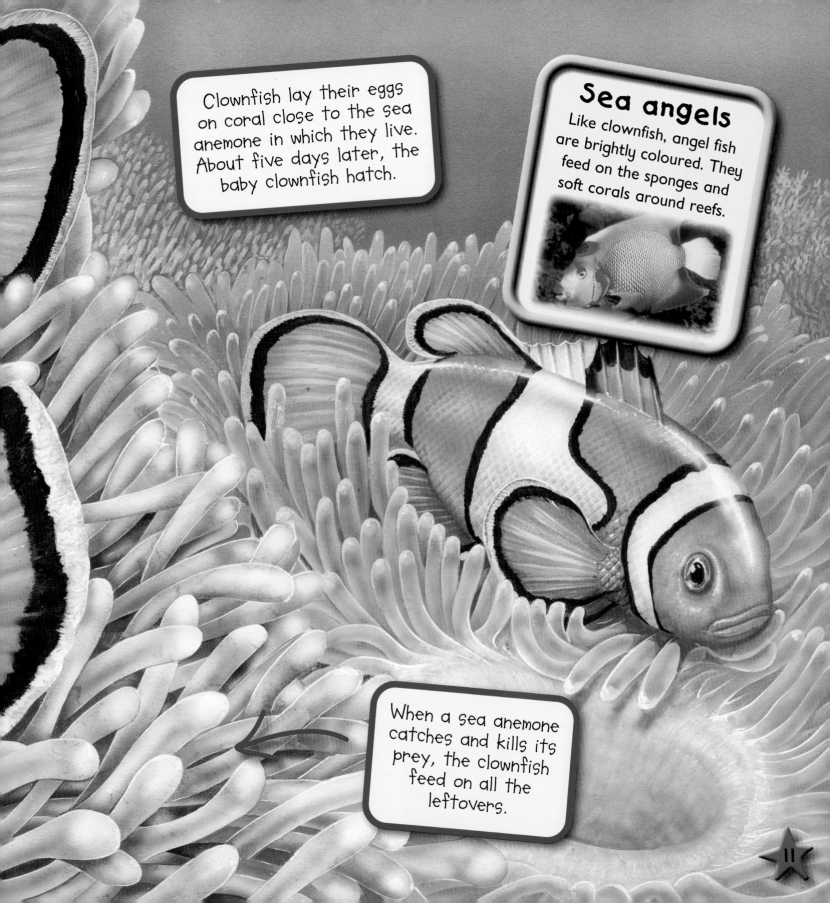

Clownfish lay their eggs on coral close to the sea anemone in which they live. About five days later, the baby clownfish hatch.

Sea angels

Like clownfish, angel fish are brightly coloured. They feed on the sponges and soft corals around reefs.

When a sea anemone catches and kills its prey, the clownfish feed on all the leftovers.

Bottlenose dolphin

If you look into a dolphin's mouth you can see why it is a member of the 'toothed whale' family. Its teeth are small and sharp to help it eat squid, octopus, eels and fish. Dolphins can often be seen following boats, leaping above the surface.

Having fun

Bottlenose dolphins love to play. They may be seen jumping out of the water then splashing back down.

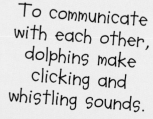

To communicate with each other, dolphins make clicking and whistling sounds.

Dolphins live in groups called schools or pods. There are usually between 10 and 25 dolphins in a group.

A young dolphin is called a calf. It will usually stay close to its mother for four or five years.

A dolphin has a blow-hole on top of its head. It uses it to breathe air at the water's surface.

13

Green turtle

Spending nearly all of their lives at sea, green turtles feed on seaweed. They swim thousands of kilometres to lay their eggs on the beach where they were born. The baby turtles hatch in the sand and then rush into the water.

The turtle's body is covered in a hard shell. This protects the turtle from hungry predators.

The back legs are used like paddles to steer the turtle as it swims. Females also use their legs to dig holes in the sand in which to lay their eggs.

14

Turtles don't have any teeth. They use their beak-shaped mouths to cut through food.

Slow going
Tortoises look like turtles but they live on land. They can only move very slowly.

The front legs are shaped like flippers to help the turtle swim. The legs are covered in large scales.

Beluga whale

These white whales are sometimes known as sea canaries. This is because they make so many squeaks and clicking noises. Belugas have beak-shaped noses but hardly any teeth. They suck small fish and squid into their mouths to eat.

The tail moves up and down, instead of side to side like a fish. This movement pushes the beluga through the water.

Whale plane
Huge white planes shaped like beluga whales are used to transport cargo that is too big for other planes.

5

A beluga calf can swim as soon as it is born. Calves are born a dark grey colour and become lighter as they grow older.

16

Belugas live in cold seas and oceans. They even swim amongst the icebergs of the Arctic Ocean.

Although they are whales, belugas are quite small — they only reach about 5 metres in length.

Flying fish

These amazing fish can glide across the ocean's surface. Flying fish don't actually fly, but they use their wing-like fins to skim across the water. They swim very fast, then leap out of the water with their fins outstretched like wings.

Spiky enemy

Swordfish attack and eat prey such as flying fish by slashing at them with their long sword-like snouts. Swordfish also eat squid.

Flying fish glide to escape from predators. These include fast-swimming fish such as tuna and swordfish.

Some types of flying fish have just two gliding fins. Other types have four.

Some flying fish can glide for up to 200 metres. That's about the length of two football pitches.

19

Manta ray

A manta ray has huge, wing-like fins. The fins can measure up to 7 metres across — longer than a minibus! As the manta ray swims, it looks like it is flying through the water. This diamond-shaped fish is the biggest type of ray.

Sea skate

A skate is a fish that looks like a ray. It swims along the seabed looking for food.

These fish are so big, only large sharks and killer whales attack them.

Giant moray eel

An eel is long and thin and looks more like a snake than a fish. The giant moray eel eats fish, squid and crabs, which it catches with its sharp teeth. It hides between rocks and shoots out to grab any passing prey.

A second set of teeth in the eel's throat help it to swallow its wriggling food.

Cleaner wrasse fish nibble at the eel's teeth to keep them clean. The eel doesn't seem to mind, and it doesn't eat the smaller fish.

The giant moray eel can grow to 4 metres long – over twice as long as a human.

Moray eels are nocturnal. This means they prefer to rest during the day and are more active at night.

Sea snake
As well as eels, there are snakes in the ocean. The yellow-bellied sea snake has a poisonous bite.

Fun facts

Great white shark If attacking their prey from beneath, great whites swim through the water at speed and may jump right out of the water.

Giant octopus A female octopus looks after her eggs until they hatch, then she dies soon afterwards.

Thorny seahorse Seahorses can move each of their eyes in different directions!

Clownfish All clownfish are born males. Some turn into females as they grow older.

Bottlenose dolphin If a dolphin is sick or injured, other members of the group help it to the surface to breathe.

Green turtle Baby turtles eat sea creatures such as fish, jellyfish and crabs. Adults only eat plants.

Beluga whale The mother's milk is full of fatty goodness to help her calf grow strong.

Flying fish Sometimes, flying fish may land on the decks of boats and yachts as they glide through the air.

Manta ray The female manta ray gives birth to a single baby, which is called a pup.

Giant moray eel The bodies of some types of moray eels are covered in poisonous slime.